LASERS AND HOLOGRAMS

This edition produced in **1993** for
Shooting Star Press Inc
230 Fifth Avenue
New York, NY 10001

Design David West
Children's Book Design

Editorial Lionheart Books

Researcher Emma Krikler

Illustrator Alex Pang

Consultant Dr. Dunstan, Surrey University

Created and produced by
Aladdin Books Ltd
28 Percy Street
London W1P 9FF

*First published in the
United States in 1991 by*
Gloucester Press

ISBN 1-56924-014-0

Printed in Belgium

CONTENTS

HOW · IT · WORKS

LASERS AND HOLOGRAMS

IAN GRAHAM

SHOOTING STAR PRESS

THE WORKING PARTS

A laser is a device used to produce an intense beam of light. A beam of laser light is very different from the ordinary light produced by an electric bulb or the sun. Lasers have three special characteristics, or scientific "properties."

Ordinary light is a mixture of many wavelengths of light traveling out in all directions from the light source. We see these wavelengths of light as different colors. When all the colors mix together they form white light. A laser beam is composed of only one wavelength. This property is called "monochromaticity." This means that the light is composed of only one color and not all the colors of the rainbow, which is known as "multichromaticity."

All the waves in a laser beam travel in the same direction and all their peaks and troughs – the upper and lower limits of the waves – line up together. This property is called "coherence."

Rays of ordinary light spread out as they travel away from their source. The rays of a laser beam spread very little. They form an almost straight path of light, called "collimation."

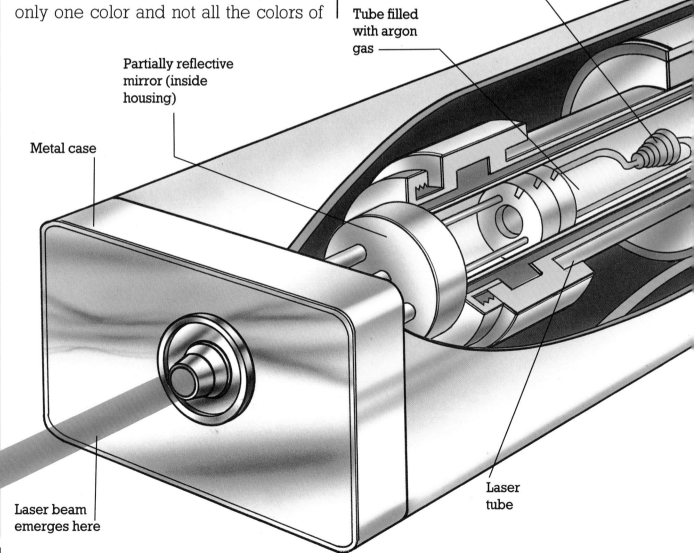

Electrode

Tube filled with argon gas

Partially reflective mirror (inside housing)

Metal case

Laser tube

Laser beam emerges here

The most important part of a laser is the material that produces the light. This is called the laser's active medium. The first lasers were made from solid materials such as the gemstone ruby. Later, liquids and gases were used too.

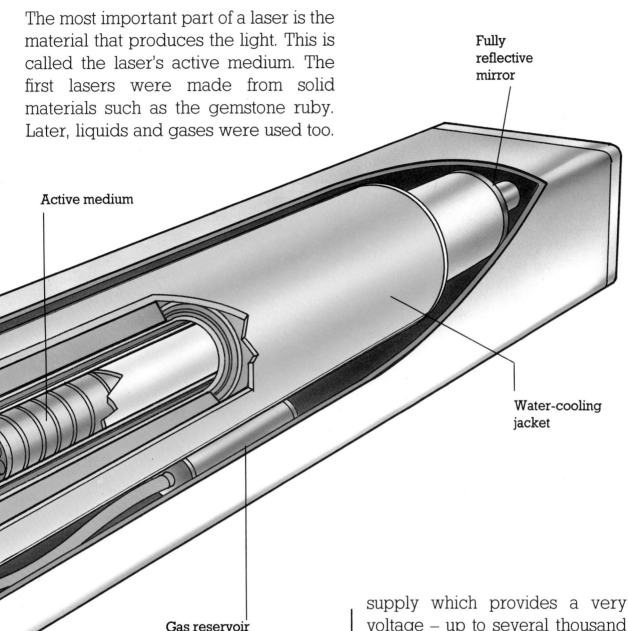

Active medium

Fully reflective mirror

Water-cooling jacket

Gas reservoir

The laser shown here is a gas laser. The active medium is a 20 in-long glass tube filled with the chosen gas. Argon, carbon dioxide and a mixture of helium and neon gases are commonly used.

The tube has an electrode, an electrical connection, at each end. The two electrodes are connected to a power supply which provides a very high voltage – up to several thousand volts. This pumps energy into the active medium and causes it to emit a strong burst of light.

At each end of the tube there is a very precisely shaped mirror. Each mirror is held in a movable clamp so that it can be adjusted to reflect light accurately along the length of the tube. One mirror is partially reflective and so allows some of the light from the tube to pass through it. This forms the intense beam of light that shines out of one end of the laser unit.

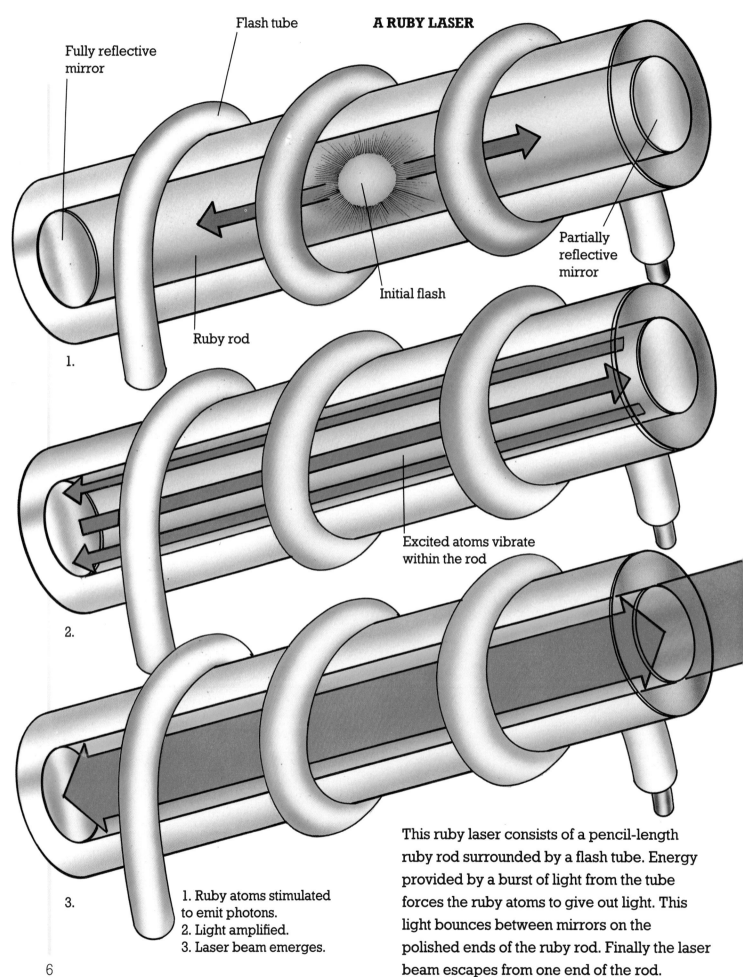

Fully reflective mirror

Flash tube

A RUBY LASER

Initial flash

Partially reflective mirror

Ruby rod

1.

Excited atoms vibrate within the rod

2.

3.

1. Ruby atoms stimulated to emit photons.
2. Light amplified.
3. Laser beam emerges.

This ruby laser consists of a pencil-length ruby rod surrounded by a flash tube. Energy provided by a burst of light from the tube forces the ruby atoms to give out light. This light bounces between mirrors on the polished ends of the ruby rod. Finally the laser beam escapes from one end of the rod.

HOW LASERS WORK

The name LASER comes from the first letters of the words which describe how it works – Light Amplification by Stimulated Emission of Radiation. A laser is a device which excites atoms, the smallest particles of the Universe, so that they give out energy as light in a special way. Follow the illustrations on the left and you can see how this happens. The laser shown here consists of a rod made of ruby crystals. This rod is set inside a cylinder with a mirror at either end. One mirror is fully reflective, but the other is only partially silvered and so a very strong light will to be able to pass through it.

A flash tube is coiled around the cylinder. When this fires a flash of light the ruby atoms inside the tube become excited and produce tiny bursts of light called photons. These photons strike the atoms, exciting them to produce more and more photons until the tube is filled with them bouncing back and forth from mirror to mirror. Soon the amount of photons is so great that they pass right through the partially reflective mirror. This is the laser beam itself.

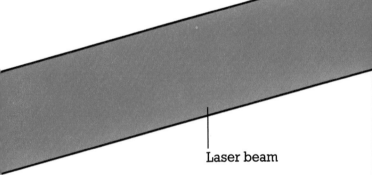

Laser beam

Ordinary light (below) consists of a random mixture of different wavelengths traveling in different directions. Laser light (below right) consists of a beam of parallel waves with their peaks and lows lined up with each other.

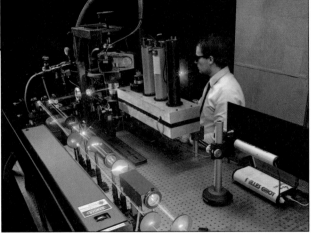

A laser in action.

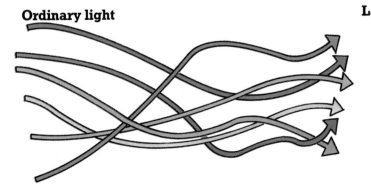

Ordinary light

Laser light

DIFFERENT TYPES

Lasers are widely used in industry, medicine and scientific research. They are divided into several groups according to the active medium – the material used to produce the beam. This may be a solid, a liquid or a gas.

The gas laser is the most popular type. The color of the light it produces depends on the gas or the mixture of gases that it contains. For example, helium-neon gas lasers produce beams of red light and argon lasers produce blue-green light. Both are used for spectacular light shows. In stores, some products have a pattern of black and white lines called a bar code printed on their packaging. By bouncing a laser beam off this, information contained in the code can be transferred to the cash register and the store's computer. The beam bounces off the white lines more strongly than off the black, producing on/off electrical signals, a digital code. Lasers are also used to produce three-dimensional images called holograms.

Small powerful lasers used in hospitals can cut like a scalpel, a surgeon's knife, and seal leaking blood vessels.

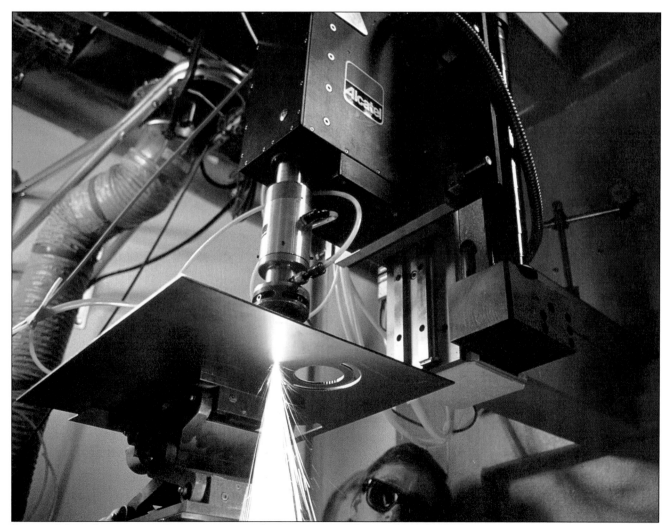

8 **Powerful and accurate lasers are used to cut materials such as this sheet of metal.**

ISBN 0-7496-0424-7

9 780749 604240

Using a solid-state laser-containing wand to read a bar code (inset) printed on a book cover.

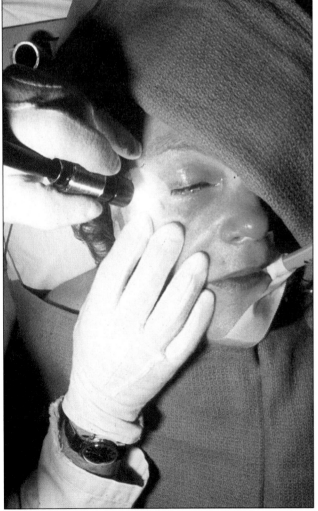

Lasers are used in healing operations.

A 3-D hologram made with a laser.

9

CUTTING AND WELDING

Several types of laser are powerful enough to cut or drill through a wide range of materials. One advantage of using a laser is that there is no metal blade or drill bit to wear out or break. Paper, cloth, plastics, ceramics and metals can all be cut by laser. Some materials that can be heated by laser to their melting points can also be joined by melting their edges together. This process is called laser welding.

The carbon dioxide gas laser is often used in industry to cut and weld steel. A jet of oxygen is sometimes directed along the laser beam to the metal. Reactions between the hot metal and the oxygen enable the laser to cut or make holes through the metal more quickly. If materials are to be cut by laser, they must be able to absorb energy from the laser beam. Materials with smooth reflective surfaces, like glass, can be cut by laser if their surface is first coated with a layer of a substance like carbon which is black and so absorbs, but does not reflect, laser radiation.

Electronic components are often connected to each other by a process called soldering. The parts to be joined are held together and a metallic material known as solder is melted around them to make a good electrical connection. Soldering is usually done with a hot soldering iron, but it can also be done by a carbon dioxide laser.

Gas lasers, like this one cutting cloth, are replacing ordinary cutting machines in industry.

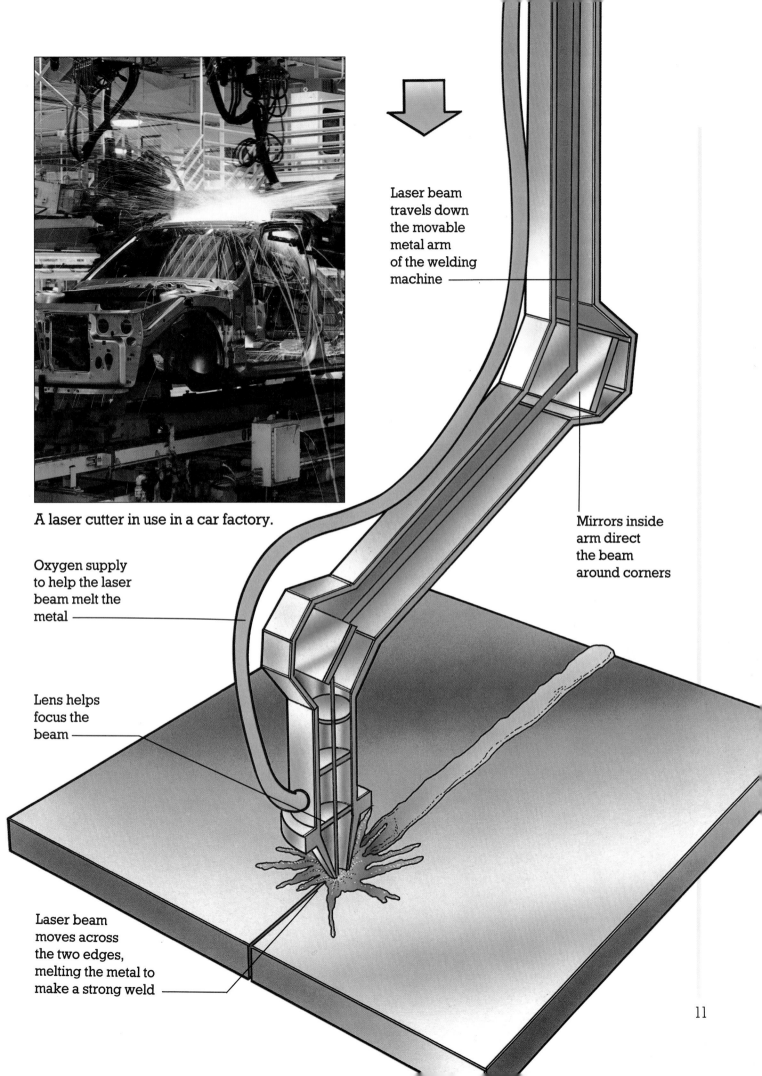

A laser cutter in use in a car factory.

Laser beam travels down the movable metal arm of the welding machine

Mirrors inside arm direct the beam around corners

Oxygen supply to help the laser beam melt the metal

Lens helps focus the beam

Laser beam moves across the two edges, melting the metal to make a strong weld

STRAIGHT AND TRUE

A laser beam travels in a straight and narrow line. Scientists and engineers make use of this "collimation" in two ways. The rodlike beams can be used to guide machinery in a straight line or to measure distances.

To measure distance, a short burst of light from a laser is directed at a target some distance away. The burst, or pulse, "bounces" back from the target like an echo. The time it takes the pulse to travel to the target and back to the laser is measured. The distance to the target, also called its range, is given by multiplying half of this time by the speed of the pulse, which travels at the speed of light (186,000mp/sec). The time is halved because the pulse travels twice the required distance.

In the building industry, lasers are used like plumb lines, spirit levels and rulers to check structures are vertical or horizontal. In forestry, laser range-finders help to measure tree height. As

A laser beam trained on fixed points ahead and behind guides this tunnel-boring machine.

an aircraft carrying a laser flies over a forest, laser pulses are fired downward. They are reflected back by the tree tops and the ground. The difference in time between the returning pulses indicates the tree height.

A laser rangefinder can also be used to detect changes in the distance between itself and its target. They have been used to register movements in the earth's surface that occur before an earthquake or volcanic eruption.

A satellite called LAGEOS helps to study the movements of land masses in the hope of predicting earthquakes, such as along the San Andreas Fault in California. Laser beams are directed at LAGEOS from points around rock faults (points A, B, C). The beams are reflected back to adjoining targets. Any changes in position of the three points reveal dangerous land movements.

Lasers at an earthquake warning center detect any movements in the earth's crust.

LAGEOS satellite positioned over the United States

Laser beams directed at and reflected back by LAGEOS

Earthquake zone

Point A

Point B

San Andreas Fault

Point C

LASERS IN MEDICINE

Medical lasers are used in three ways: to cut like a scalpel, to destroy cells by heating, and to join cells together. When a cut is made with a scalpel, the open ends of blood vessels bleed into the cut. The advantage of using a laser instead of a scalpel is that the laser beam seals blood vessels as it cuts through them and the cut remains dry. Carbon dioxide lasers can be used for this and also for destroying harmful cancer cells by heating them quickly so that they burst or turn to vapor.

Several types of laser are used for medical welding, called "coagulation." The blue-green light from an argon laser passes through clear watery cells without any effect, but it is absorbed by brown skin cells or red blood cells underneath. Wounds can be healed without using bandages and stitches.

An Nd-YAG laser, a solid-state laser, produces light in the near-infrared. This is absorbed by most dark cells whatever their color and so it can treat cells that cannot be treated by an argon laser. A carbon dioxide laser beam is powerful and full of heat-energy so it affects *all* the cells it strikes.

Laser surgery

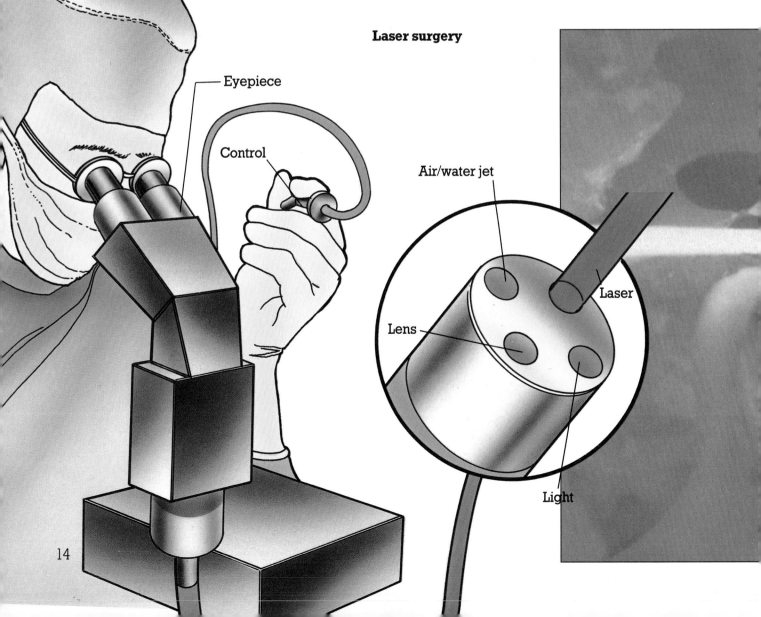

Eyepiece

Control

Air/water jet

Laser

Lens

Light

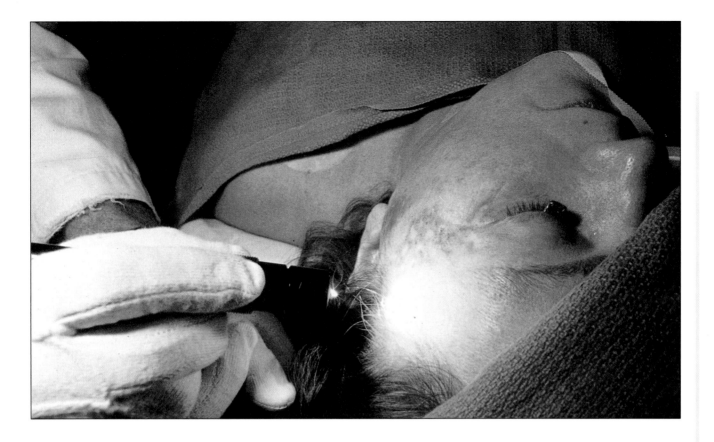

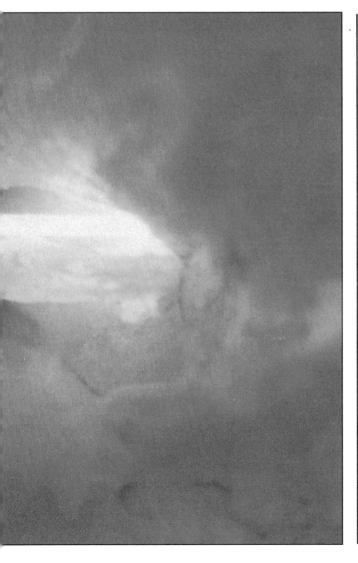

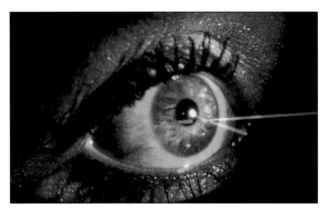

(Left) Laser surgery can be carried out inside the body. The laser beam is sent along a flexible fiber optic cable passed down the patient's windpipe.

(Top) Argon lasers are used to remove red marks on the skin called port-wine stains. The beam destroys the cells of the birthmark and seals the surrounding cells.

(Above) Leaking blood vessels inside the eye that may blur vision or cause blindness are sealed by laser surgery. If the light-sensitive part of the eye, the retina, becomes torn, the patient's sight can be saved by welding the retina in place by laser.

VISION AND SOUND

Visual information about an object can be obtained by firing a laser beam at the object and studying the reflection coming back from it. The fact that there *is* a reflection shows that an object lies ahead. The time taken for the reflection to arrive gives the object's range. The bright and dark pattern of the reflection contains information about the object's size and shape. This can be used to reject unwanted items from objects moving along a factory conveyor belt.

Information can be stored on a disc as a spiral track of shallow pits burned into the mirrored disc. If a laser beam is bounced off the disc, it is reflected by the shiny surface but not by the pits. The reflections picked up by a detector form a series of pulses which are converted back into the original information used to make the disc. One type of laser disc, called a compact disc, uses this method to store high-quality music. Another type, a video disc, stores visual information – photographic images and maps.

Objects passing along a conveyor belt (right) can be sorted by a laser system. A laser is positioned above the belt. Objects that pass along the belt are illuminated by the beam and reflect it up to a scanner. Identical objects should produce identical reflections. The system can be programmed to reject objects when the scanner does not receive the correct pattern or strength of reflection. Objects can be removed from the conveyor belt by triggering an electrically operated push rod or by a puff of high-pressure air to shift the object sideways off the belt. Such automatic sorting systems are used in factories.

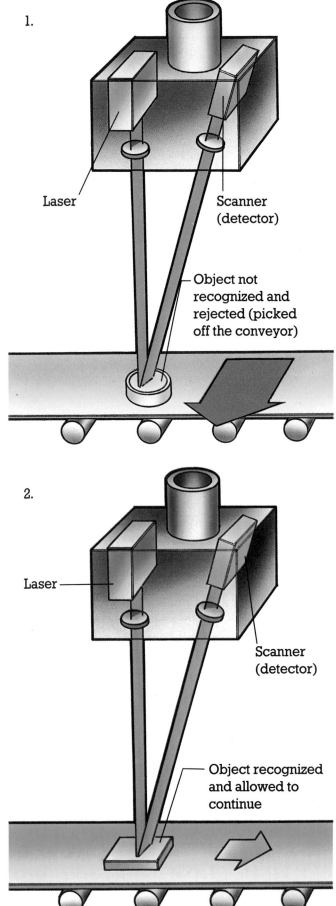

1.

Laser

Scanner (detector)

Object not recognized and rejected (picked off the conveyor)

2.

Laser

Scanner (detector)

Object recognized and allowed to continue

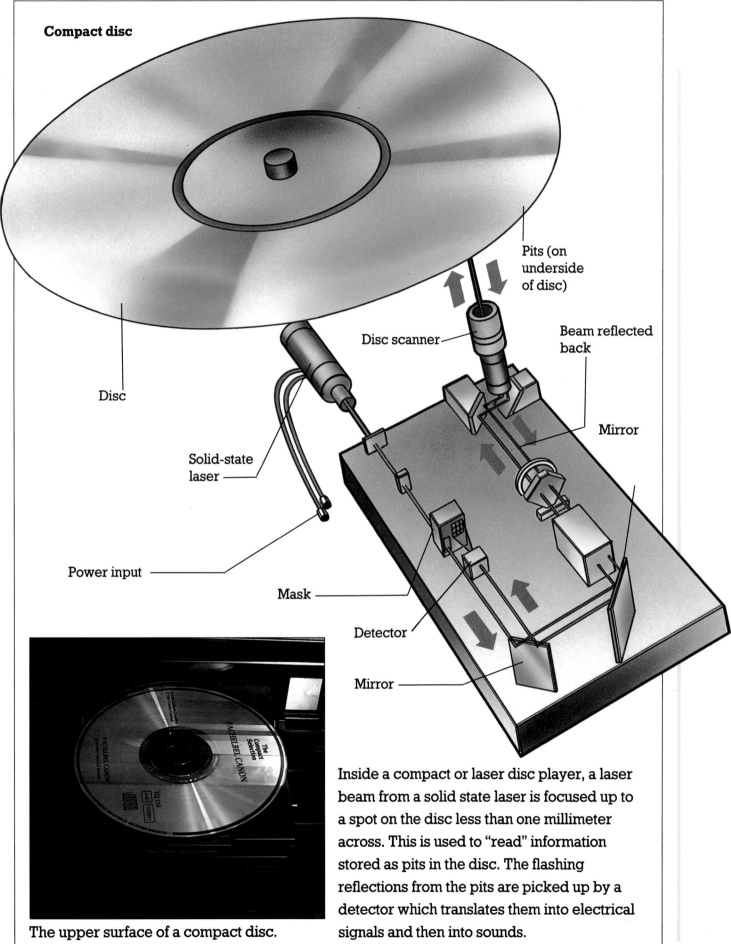

Compact disc

Pits (on underside of disc)

Disc scanner

Beam reflected back

Mirror

Disc

Solid-state laser

Power input

Mask

Detector

Mirror

The upper surface of a compact disc.

Inside a compact or laser disc player, a laser beam from a solid state laser is focused up to a spot on the disc less than one millimeter across. This is used to "read" information stored as pits in the disc. The flashing reflections from the pits are picked up by a detector which translates them into electrical signals and then into sounds.

17

COMMUNICATIONS LINK

Normal glass, for example that used in window panes, contains various chemicals which increasingly prevent light from passing through as the glass is made thicker. In the 1960s scientists began to investigate the possibility of communicating by sending information in the form of a beam of light along long, fine strands of glass called optical fibers. At that time, glass pure enough to make long strands through which light would travel did not exist. Neither did a sufficiently small but powerful light source. Both were developed in the 1970s.

The world's purest glass had to be made to carry the light beams over distances of many miles. Lasers the size of a grain of salt were developed as the small, powerful light sources. Each was made from a tiny chip of a material known as a semiconductor and placed at the transmitting end of an optical fiber. Many fibers are grouped in a cable. An optical cable can carry more than ten times as many telephone calls as a metal cable of the same thickness. Optical cables do not suffer from the electrical noise that can make a telephone call hard to hear. It is also difficult to "tap" an optical cable – that is, to listen in to someone else's telephone calls. The line-tapper would have to break the optical cable and this can be easily detected.

Also, all forms of communications, including voice, music, computer data, photographs, text and drawings, can be sent along the same optical cable; and sand, the raw material for making optical fibers, is very cheap and plentiful.

A telephone caller's voice, picked up by a microphone, is converted into a series of electrical pulses represented by ones and zeros – a digital signal (left). These turn a laser on and off, sending thousands of light pulses along an optical fiber every second. The fiber's outer layer reflects light like a mirror, preventing it from escaping from the fiber. At the receiving telephone, the digital signal is decoded and used to vibrate a thin sheet, or diaphragm, to recreate the caller's voice.

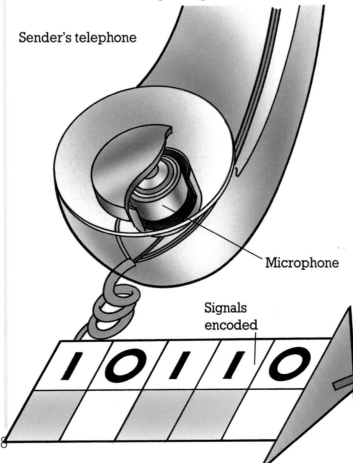

Sender's telephone

Microphone

Signals encoded

Optical fiber

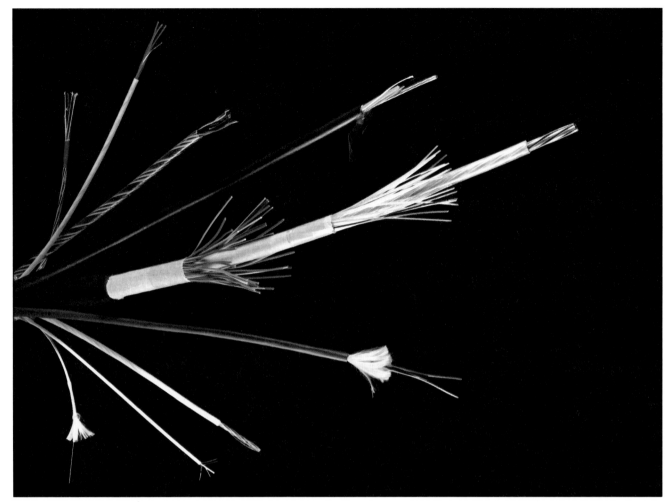

Bunches of flexible strands of glass like these are rapidly replacing metal telephone cables.

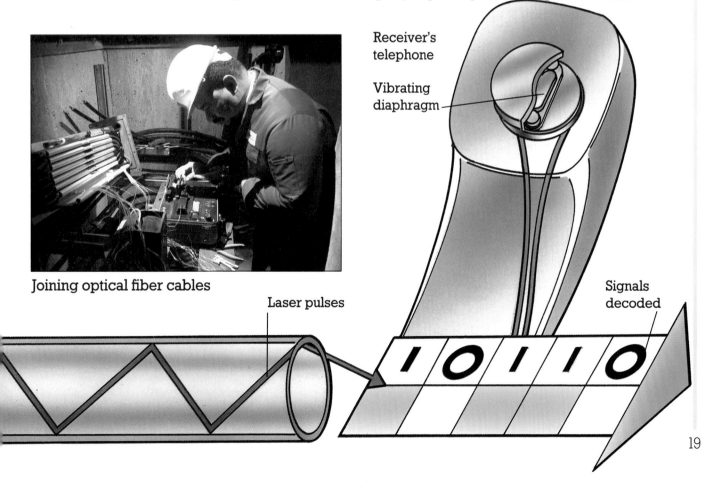

Joining optical fiber cables

Receiver's
telephone

Vibrating
diaphragm

Laser pulses

Signals
decoded

IN SPACE AND WAR

Space lasers and military lasers are now used for rangefinding, identifying targets and communications. They are to be found as rangefinders for tanks and guns and bombs to indicate precisely how far away targets are. Scientists have even used lasers to measure the distance between the earth and the moon.

Some missiles are designed to fly toward laser radiation. If a laser beam is trained on a target, a missile can pick up the beam's reflection and fly along it toward the target. Secret military messages are transmitted using lasers, because it is very difficult to listen in to a laser beam carrying messages or computer data without being detected.

There have also been plans to use large high-power lasers as weapons, but there are problems with this. Experiments show that the air around the beam heats up, spreading the beam and reducing its effectiveness. When the beam strikes, say, a tank, a small area of metal turns to vapor and forms a cloud that prevents the beam from getting through to cause more damage.

The crews of American spacecraft Apollo 11, 14 and 15 each positioned a laser reflector on the moon. Each consisted of 100 individual reflectors arranged in a square frame 46 centimeters (17.9 inches) across. They reflected laser pulses fired from ruby lasers at the Lick Observatory, California, and the McDonald Observatory, Texas. Lasers are also used as rangefinders on a variety of weapons, from rifles to 60-ton tanks (far right). These are usually miniature battery-powered infrared lasers.

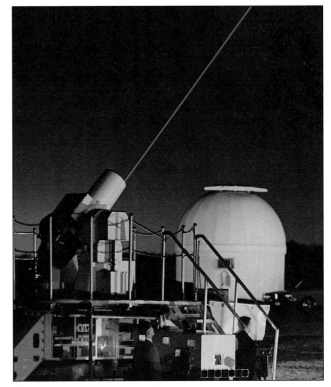
A laser aimed at a reflector on the moon.

A laser rangefinder mounted on a field gun.

A group of soldiers (below right) has discovered an enemy tank. They fire their portable laser at it and call up a missile launcher by radio. From a hidden position it fires a laser-guided missile. High above the battlefield, the missile detects laser radiation being reflected up into the sky from the target (inset). It turns and descends toward the target. The missile follows the target as long as the soldiers illuminate it with their laser. The beam travels in a straight line from the laser to the target, so there is no danger of the missile attacking the soldiers firing the laser. However, the enemy tank may "see" with its sensors that it has been made a target by the beam. It can call up forces to wipe out the soldiers or even to send up an antimissile missile.

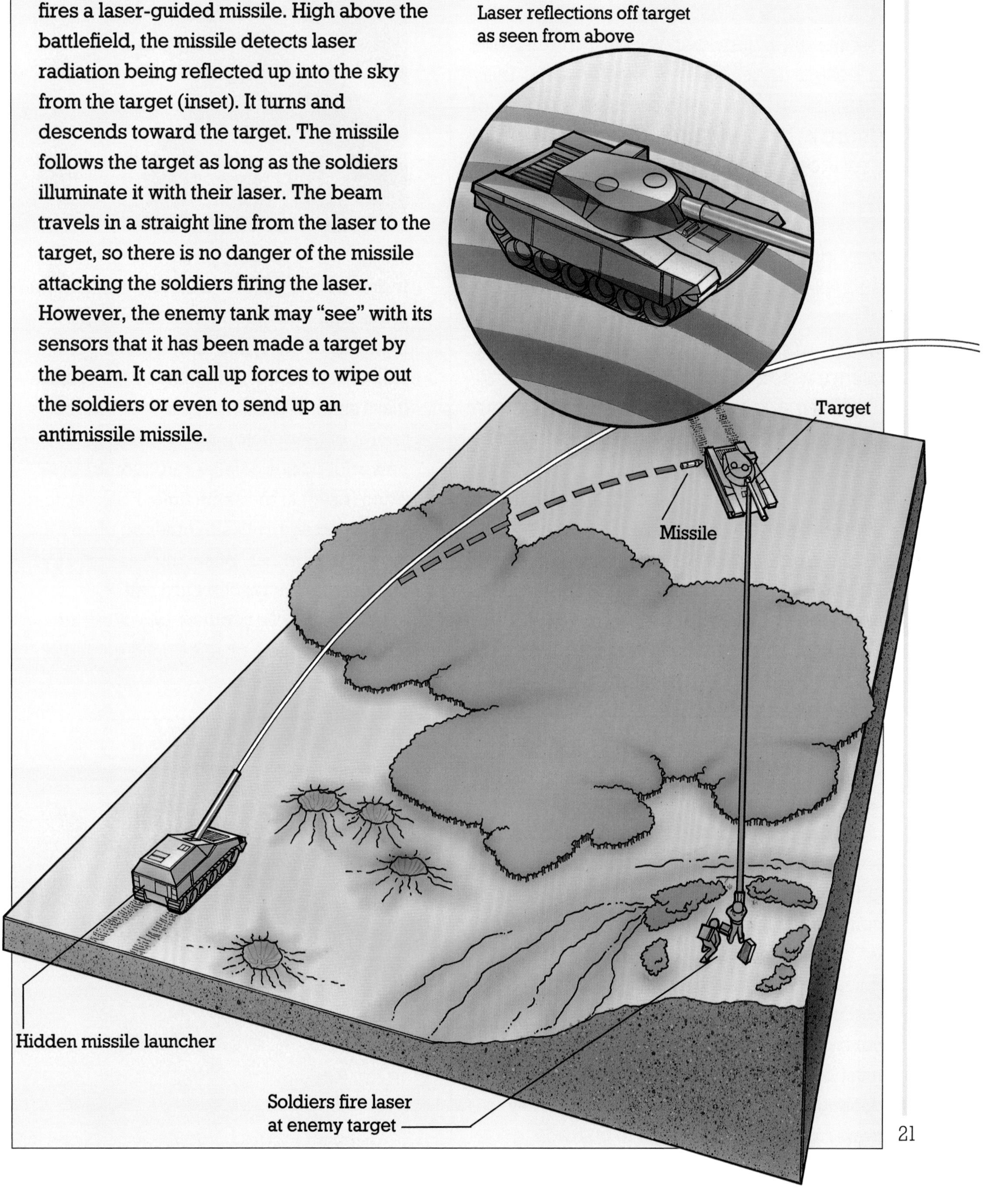

Laser reflections off target as seen from above

Target

Missile

Hidden missile launcher

Soldiers fire laser at enemy target

OTHER USES

The enormous amount of energy produced by stars like the sun is the result of a process called nuclear fusion. In the center of a star, particles of matter are pressed together so tightly that they fuse, heat up and release bursts of energy. In the future, scientists hope to produce power from nuclear fusion here on earth. The fuel must be compressed as if it were inside a star. One way of producing such huge pressures and temperatures is the controlled firing of lasers at the fuel. This heats it suddenly to millions of °F, which helps to compress it.

When a laser is fired through the air, particles of matter in the atmosphere reflect, or scatter, a small part of the beam to the sides. The more particles there are, the more the beam is scattered. A detector can register the fall in strength of the beam. This is how lasers are used to monitor air pollution. Another important development for the future is the optical computer, using laser beams instead of metal wires to carry information at the speed of light.

Lasers are used in automatic sorting systems to ensure components fit in place (right). They are also used at pop concerts as visual entertainment (far right). The speed of a computer is limited by the speed at which information moves within it. Information moves at the speed of light in an optical computer. The most powerful ordinary computers produce so much heat that they must be cooled. Light beams do not require cooling. Lasers may therefore enable very powerful optical computers to be made.

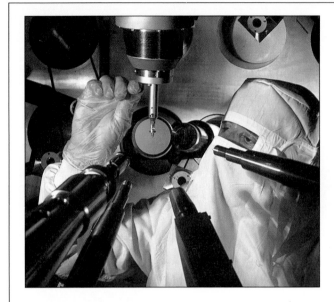

Inside a laser fusion reactor. A pellet of fuel is injected into the reactor (above). It is made up of two types of hydrogen gas called deuterium and tritium sealed inside a glass shell. When the pellet reaches the center of the reactor, it is struck by powerful pulses of laser radiation from all sides (right) at the same time. Fuel particles are forced against each other so tightly that they fuse together, releasing heat energy. But laser fusion reactors are still experimental. To produce lots of energy, millions of pellets must be used each day.

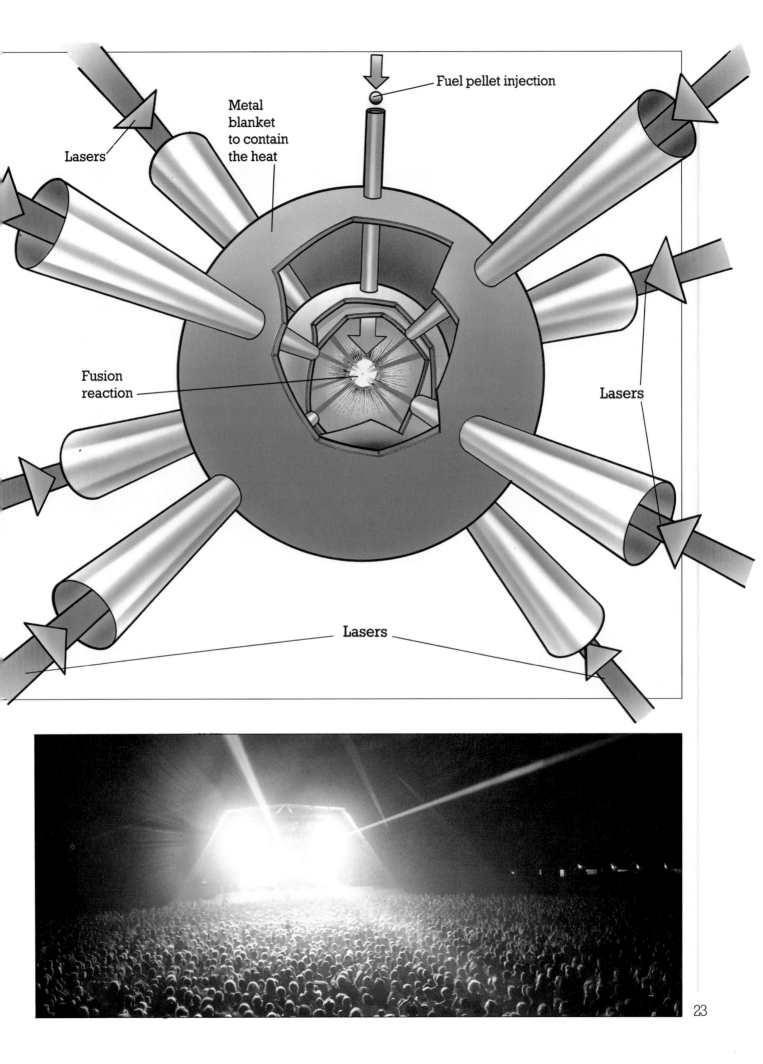

Fuel pellet injection

Metal
blanket
to contain
the heat

Lasers

Fusion
reaction

Lasers

Lasers

HOLOGRAPHY

Laser light allowed a new type of image to be invented. Holograms, as they are called, are three-dimensional (3-D) images, quite different from the two-dimensional (2-D) pictures we see in a photograph or painting. Holograms look more "real" because you can see the sides or even the back of the object shown if you move in front of it. In a 2-D image, everything is flat and looks much the same from every angle. There are two ways to make holograms. The first, called a "transmission" hologram, is lit from behind and can only be viewed in laser light. The "reflection" type of hologram is an improvement. It uses a laser to light the subject from the front, and then it can be seen in ordinary light.

Now you see it, now you don't

The two pictures (top right) show how a hologram can store surprises. (These are reflection holograms.) Looked at from the front you see a magician's hand. Move to one side and balls appear between the fingers. The hologram is really two pictures in one thanks to the shutter mechanism which allowed them to be recorded one after the other on the same plate by the laser's light.

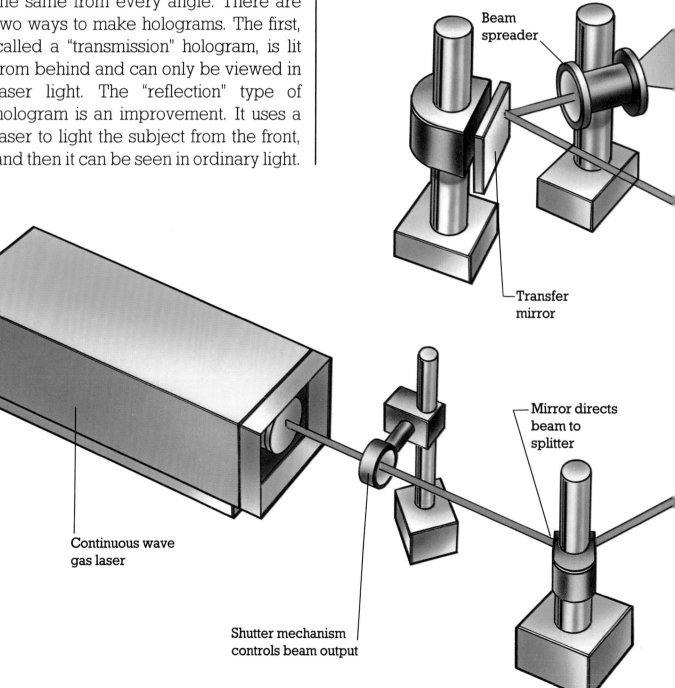

Beam spreader

Transfer mirror

Mirror directs beam to splitter

Continuous wave gas laser

Shutter mechanism controls beam output

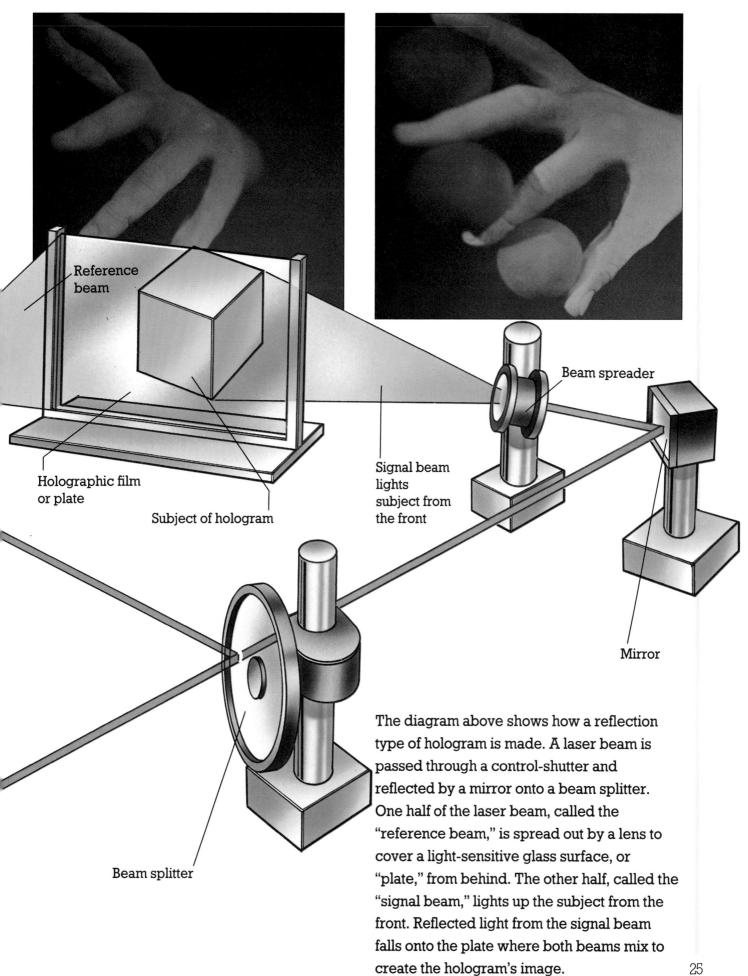

Reference beam

Holographic film or plate

Subject of hologram

Signal beam lights subject from the front

Beam spreader

Mirror

Beam splitter

The diagram above shows how a reflection type of hologram is made. A laser beam is passed through a control-shutter and reflected by a mirror onto a beam splitter. One half of the laser beam, called the "reference beam," is spread out by a lens to cover a light-sensitive glass surface, or "plate," from behind. The other half, called the "signal beam," lights up the subject from the front. Reflected light from the signal beam falls onto the plate where both beams mix to create the hologram's image.

USING HOLOGRAMS

Holograms are used in three main ways: as an art form, to record information, and as a security measure to prevent something being copied. Some shops now specialize in selling holographic works. Holograms have even been added to the exhibitions of painting and sculpture in major art galleries.

One of the most important uses of holograms in the future will be to store information. The 3-D image in a hologram contains much more detail than a normal photograph. It can be turned to show parts of the image that are normally hidden and to reveal how different objects or parts of objects relate to each other in space. Information can also be recorded in a hologram in the on-off binary code computers use.

Until recently, holograms were only made in laboratories in small numbers and they could only be viewed in laser light. Today, holograms can be made in large numbers and they can be seen in daylight. Because of this, holograms will become common in packaging, store windows and street signs.

Although holograms can be made more easily now by specialist companies, they are still almost impossible to copy. This is why they are printed onto security items, for instance credit and identity cards. In this way, holograms help to prevent fraud.

Holograms like this bird are often printed on credit cards to make it difficult to copy them.

Science has helped to create the new visual art forms of our age – photography, movies, television and now holography (as seen in the gallery above). Holograms are increasingly being used to record 3-D images of complex objects. Designers and architects can now produce holograms which show how their work will look from computer programs, and dentists can keep holographic records of patients' teeth or dental plates (below).

Information stored as holograms

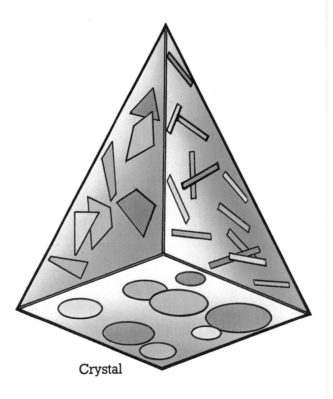

Crystal

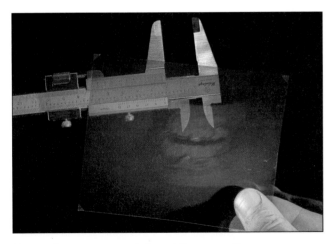

Crystals are materials with a regular geometrical shape formed from sheets (or planes) of particles. Some crystals can store a different hologram on each plane. In 1969, the U.S. Bell Laboratories found that 1,000 holograms could be stored in a crystal of lithium niobate. As the crystal is tilted, the hologram on each plane appears.

HISTORY OF LASERS

Between 1910 and 1920, discoveries made by scientists including Albert Einstein suggested that atoms could be made to give out radiation under certain conditions. Scientists were unable to prove that these theories would work in reality until the technology to test their ideas became available in the 1950s.

In 1953, while working at Columbia University in the United States, Dr. Charles Townes built a device called a maser. Its name was formed from the first letters of Microwave Amplification by Stimulated Emission of Radiation. Townes' maser produced an intense beam of radio waves from ammonia gas. More masers were built in the 1950s.

Albert Einstein studied light and atoms.

In 1958, Charles Townes and Arthur Schawlow suggested that masers could be made to produce light instead of radio waves. The first of these devices was made in 1960 by Theodore Maiman. It used a ruby rod surrounded by a flash tube. A burst of light from the flash tube produced an intense pulse of light from

Theodore Maiman with one of his lasers.

the ends of the rod. After the ruby maser came development of the helium-neon gas maser in 1961. Other gas masers followed. Scientists then began looking for ways of making solid-state masers from semiconductor materials. The first of these, the gallium arsenide maser, was developed in 1962.

All these new types of light-producing devices were called optical masers until 1965. Since then, they have been known as lasers from the first letters of Light Amplification by Stimulated Emission of Radiation.

The laser provided the pure, intense light needed to produce holograms.

Portrait – in a mirror and a hologram.

The first holograms had been made in the 1940s, but they were small and dim since a sufficiently powerful light source with the special properties of a laser beam was not available. The laser made it possible to make much larger and clearer holograms. Interest in holograms grew. Scientist Emmeth Leith in the United States made the first holographic movie in the 1960s. Full-color holograms were produced soon after.

When the laser was invented, it was thought to be merely an interesting scientific oddity with no practical use.

Development of new laser technology.

Since then, important uses have been found for lasers. These include industrial cutting, welding and drilling, eye surgery, cancer treatment, communications, pollution monitoring and nuclear fusion research.

In 1988, the world's first transatlantic optical fiber cable began service, carrying 40,000 simultaneous telephone messages by laser between Britain and France and the United States. In 1991, laser-guided missiles were first used on a large-scale by the coalition forces and Iraq in the Gulf War.

FACTS AND FIGURES

The first commercially built laser was made in 1961 by Trion Instruments in the United States and sold to the U.S. company Texas Instruments.

The first hologram was made in 1948, long before lasers were available, by the Hungarian-born scientist Dennis Gabor while carrying out research for the Rugby Electrical Company in Scotland. His light source was a mercury lamp. He received the Nobel Prize for Physics for his work.

The first laser holograms were made in 1961 by Emmett Leith and Juris Upatnieks at the University of Michigan.

Lasers were first used in surgery in 1963.

The first hologram of a human being was made by L. D. Siebert of the U.S. Conductron Corporation in 1966.

Lasers were used to cut cloth for the first time when in 1973 the British clothing manufacturer, John Collier, used a carbon dioxide laser to cut out cloth to make suits.

The brightest artificial light was produced by a laser at the U.S. Los Alamos National Laboratory in New Mexico in 1987.

The first compact disc to sell one million copies was *Brothers in Arms* by the rock group Dire Straits in 1986.

GLOSSARY

amplify
To increase in strength.

atom
One of the tiny particles of which all matter is made up.

coherence
A property of laser light in which all the peaks and lows of its waves line up, reinforcing each other.

dye laser
A type of laser made from a colored liquid called a dye. The dye produces a laser beam when it is energized by a flash lamp or another laser.

electromagnetic spectrum
The range of frequencies and wavelengths of electromagnetic energy. The lowest frequencies (longest wavelengths) correspond to radio waves, the highest frequencies (shortest wavelengths) to gamma rays.

excimer laser
A type of laser. Its name is formed from "excited dimer." A dimer is a substance composed of two identical molecules. Excimer lasers emit ultraviolet radiation. They are used in nuclear fuel processing and medicine.

frequency
The number of cycles or vibrations of a wave that pass a point every second. Frequency is measured in hertz (1 vibration per second = 1 hertz). Light waves to which our eyes are sensitive range in frequency between 400 million million and 750 million million hertz.

gas laser
Any laser that produces a laser beam from a gas or mixture of gases. Argon, carbon dioxide and a mixture of helium and neon are common laser gases.

hologram
A three-dimensional (3-D) image on a flat photographic film or plate using laser light as the means of illumination.

lidar
Light Detection and Ranging. A system for detecting objects and measuring how far away they are by bouncing a laser beam off them.

light knife
Another name for a laser used for cutting by a surgeon.

monochromatic
Electromagnetic energy of one wavelength only. Monochromatic light consists of light of one color only.

photon
The smallest amount of electromagnetic energy that can exist; a packet of light.

pulse
In physics, a very short burst of energy such as the mass of photons given off suddenly by the active medium of a laser when excited.

pumping

The process of injecting energy into a laser to make it work. Some lasers are optically pumped by a flash tube. Others, such as gas lasers, are electrically pumped by passing a current through the laser medium.

ruby laser

An example of a solid-state laser made from a ruby rod with a flash tube wrapped around it.

semiconductor laser

A laser made from a chip of semiconductor material such as gallium arsenide. A semiconductor acts as if in between a conductor, which allows electricity to pass, and an insulator, which prevents electricity passing. They are also called injection lasers.

solid-state

Any device in which the active parts are solids. A solid-state laser usually has a rod of crystals as the light-producing material.

watt

A standard unit of power used to measure the amount of energy created by a laser every second. Laser power ouputs range from tenths of a watt up to thousands of watts.

wavelength

The distance between the peaks of a wave motion . The wavelength of visible light is 0.4 to 0.7 millionths of a meter.

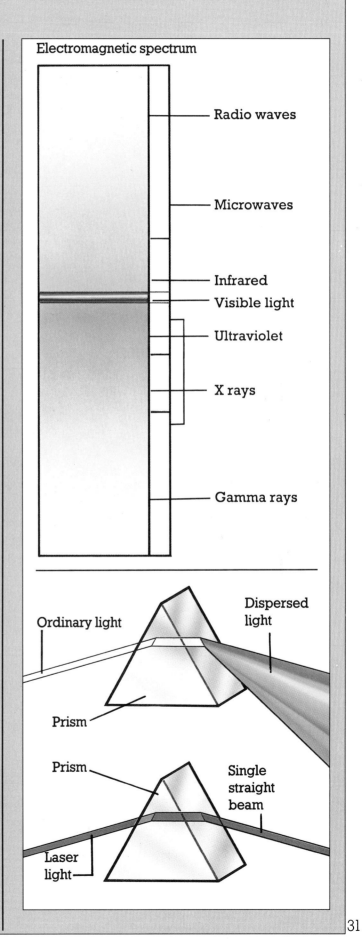

Electromagnetic spectrum

Radio waves

Microwaves

Infrared

Visible light

Ultraviolet

X rays

Gamma rays

Ordinary light

Dispersed light

Prism

Prism

Single straight beam

Laser light

INDEX

Photographic credits
Cover and pages 6, 7 left and right, 10, 13, 14-15, 15 top and bottom, 22, 23, 27 top, 28 top and bottom, 29: Science Photo Library; pages 7 top, 17, 25 left and right and 26: Roger Vlitos; page 12: QA Photos; page 19 top: STL Designs; page 19 bottom: Mercury Communications Ltd; pages 20 top and 22-23: Zefa Picture Library; pages 20 bottom: Frank Spooner Pictures; page 28 middle: Popperfoto.

PRINTED IN BELGIUM BY

proost
INTERNATIONAL BOOK PRODUCTION